# damien rice o

guitar tablature vocal

© 2005 by Faber Music Ltd
First published in 2004 by International Music Publications Ltd, a Faber Music company
3 Queen Square, London, WC1N 3AU

Arranging and engraving: Artemis Music Ltd (www.artemismusic.com)
Printed in England by Caligraving Ltd
All rights reserved

ISBN 0-571-52452-4

# delicate

Words and Music by Damien Rice

3

4

7

Outro:

# volcano

Words and Music by Damien Rice

*Intro:*

♩ = 160

Verse:

1. Don't hold your-self_____ like that,
2. Don't throw your-self_____ like that,

*w/light palm muting*

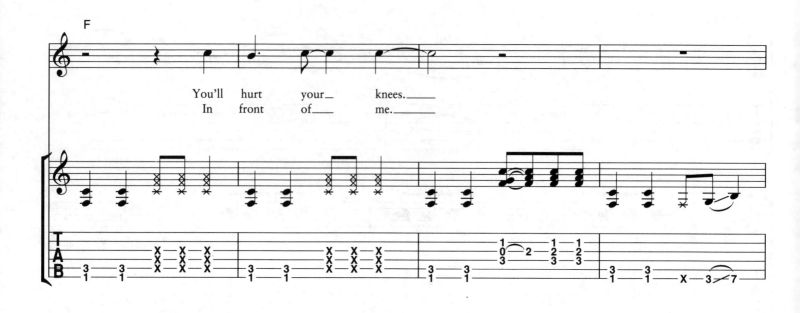

You'll hurt your_ knees._
In front of_ me._

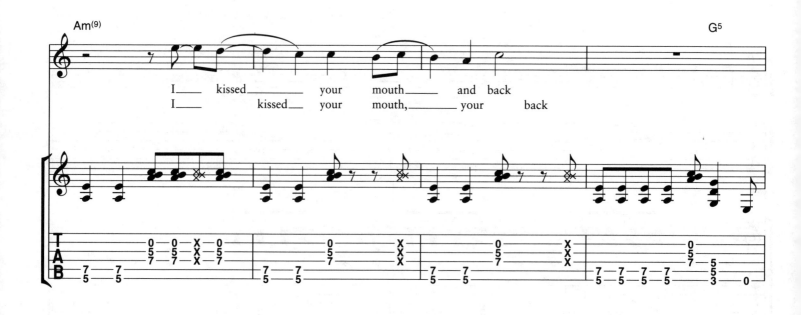

I_ kissed_ your mouth_ and back
I_ kissed_ your mouth,_ your back

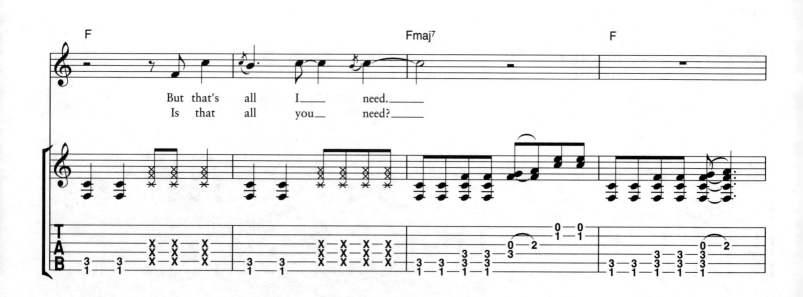

But that's all I_ need._
Is that all you_ need?_

*Bridge:*

*Outro:*

*Play 4 times*

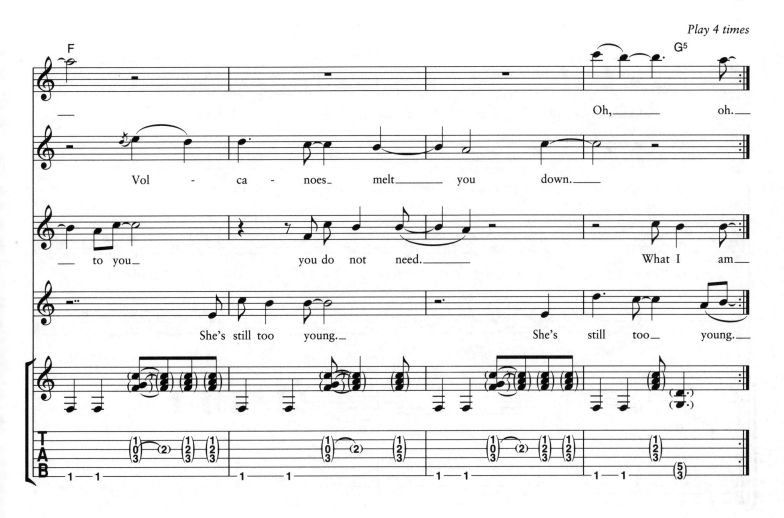

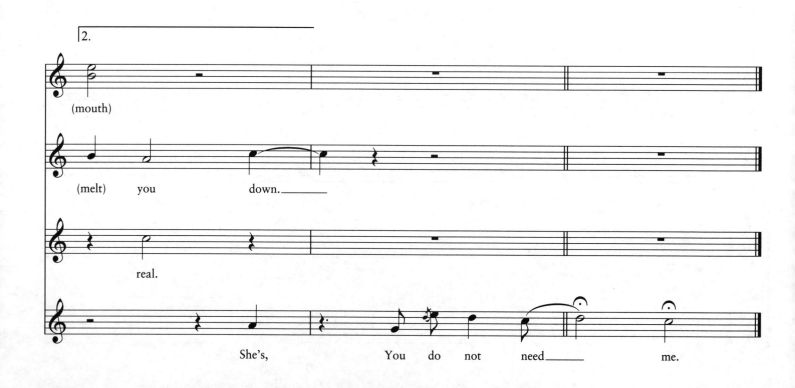

# the blower's daughter

Words and Music by Damien Rice

The shor - ter sto - ry.
The col - der wa - ter.

Gtr 2. *(2° only)*

Cello arr. for Gtr.

*mp*

No love no glo - ry.
The blo - wer's daugh - ter.

22

# cannonball

Words and Music by Damien Rice

To Coda ⊕

Verse

Gtr. 1

w/Fig. 1 (Acous. Gtrs. 2+3)

There's still a lit-tle bit of your taste___ in my mouth. There's still a lit-tle bit of you laced_

___ with my doubt. It's still a lit-tle hard_ to say___ what's go -

Stones taught me to fly.___ Love taught me to cry.___

___ So come on cou - rage, teach me to be shy._____ 'Cause it's not hard

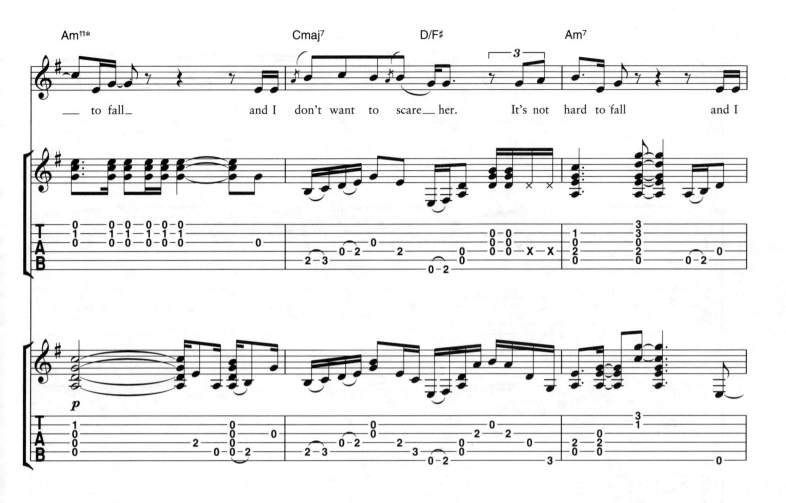

to fall and I don't want to scare her. It's not hard to fall and I

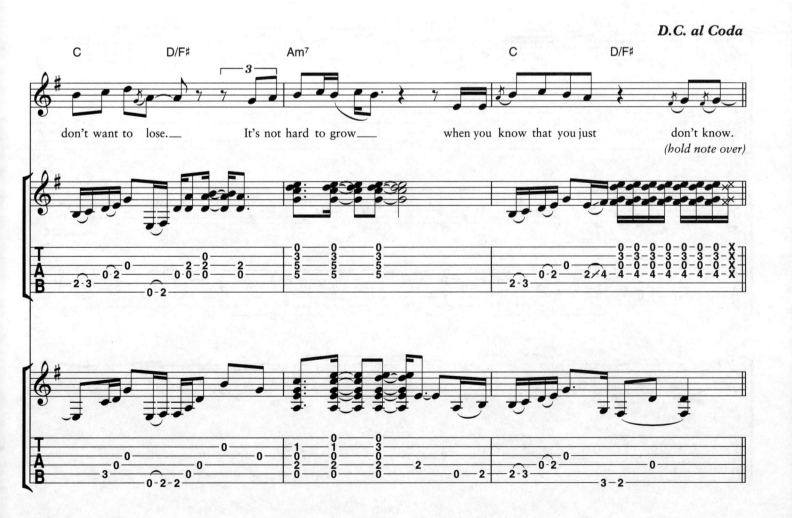

*D.C. al Coda*

don't want to lose. It's not hard to grow when you know that you just don't know.
*(hold note over)*

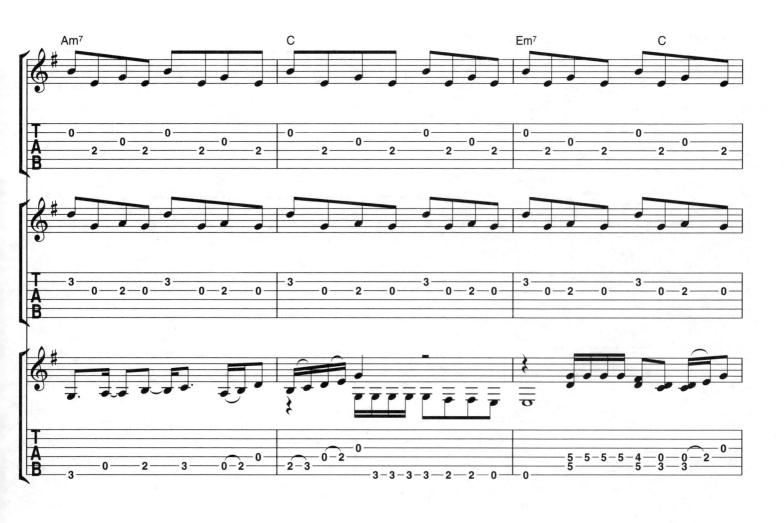

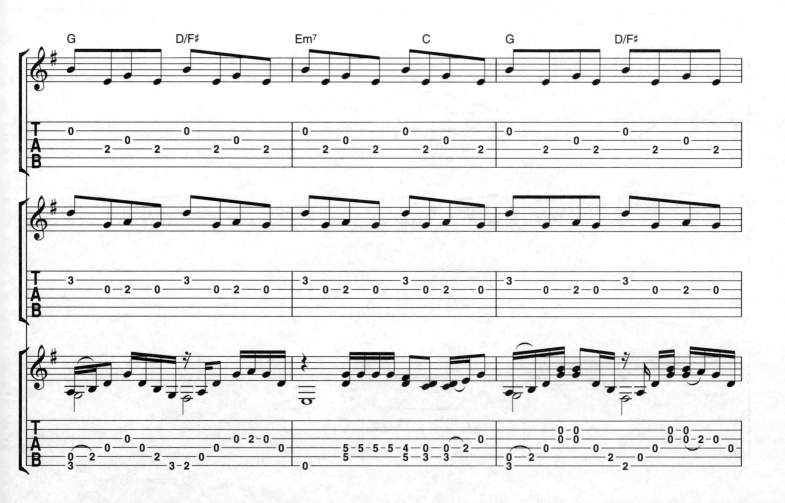

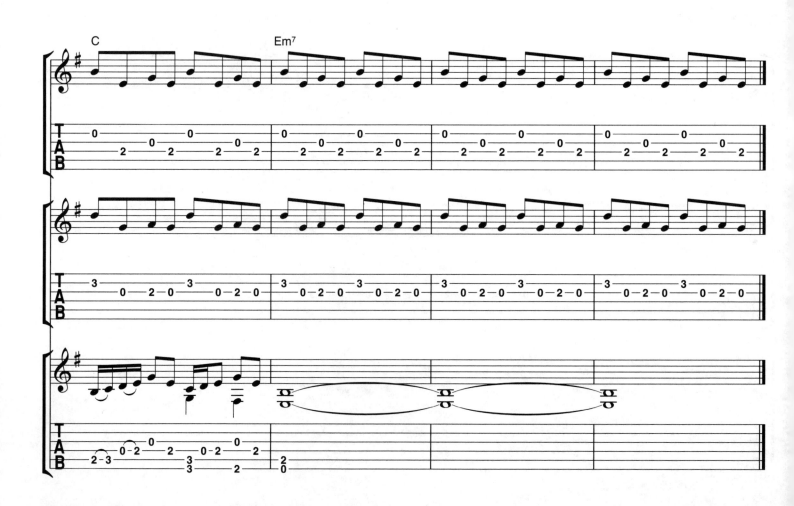

# older chests

Words and Music by Damien Rice

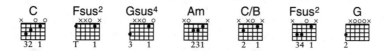

$\quad$ = 112

Acous. Gtr. 1

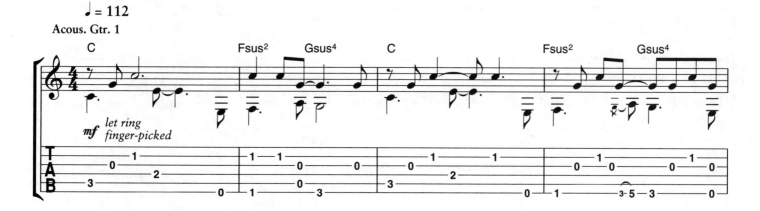

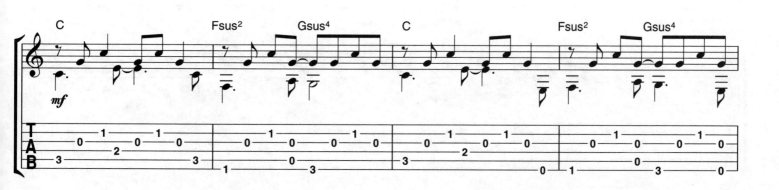

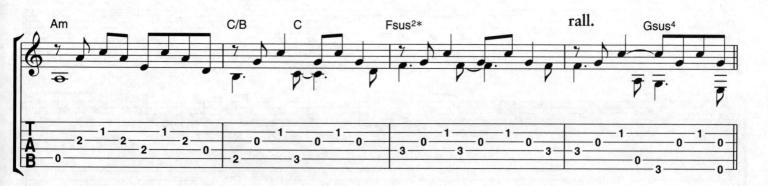

*Verse:*

**a tempo**

Pre-chorus:

*Chorus:*

# amie

Words and Music by Damien Rice

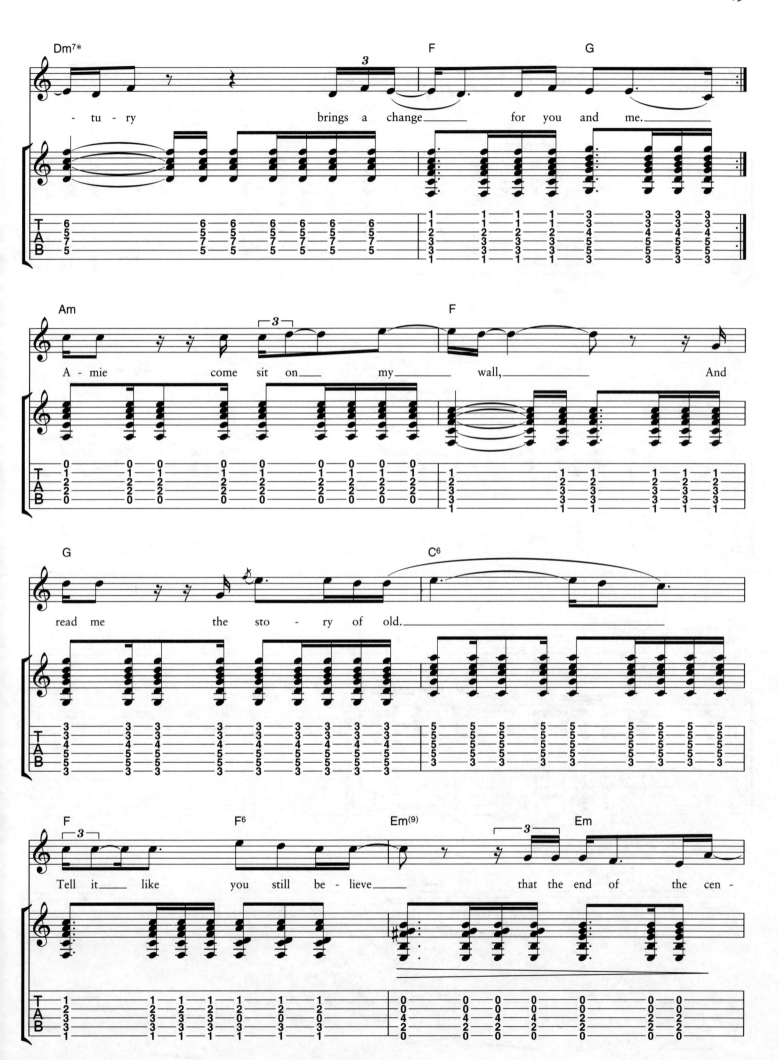

# cheers darlin'

Words and Music by Damien Rice

Cheers,___ dar - lin',  I got your___ wed - ding bells___ in my ear.
Cheers,___ dar - lin',  I got a___ rib - bon of green on my gui - tar.

**Acous. Gtr. 1**

**Acous. Gtr. 2**

*2° only...*
*composite part*

Cheers,___ dar - lin',___  you gave me three cig - ar - rettes to___ smoke my___ tears a - way.
Cheers,___ dar - lin',___  I got a beau - ty queen, to sit not ve - ry far from me.

*Interlude*

# cold water

Words and Music by Damien Rice

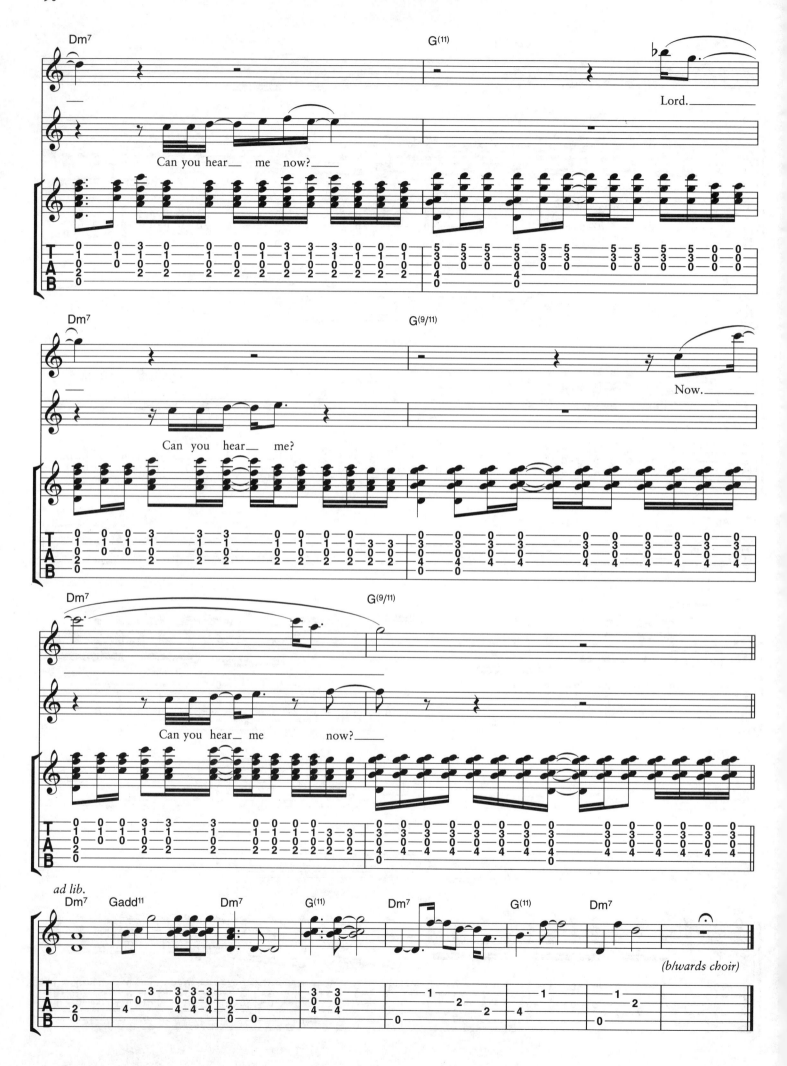

# i remember

Words and Music by Damien Rice

58

60

* Use T on 6

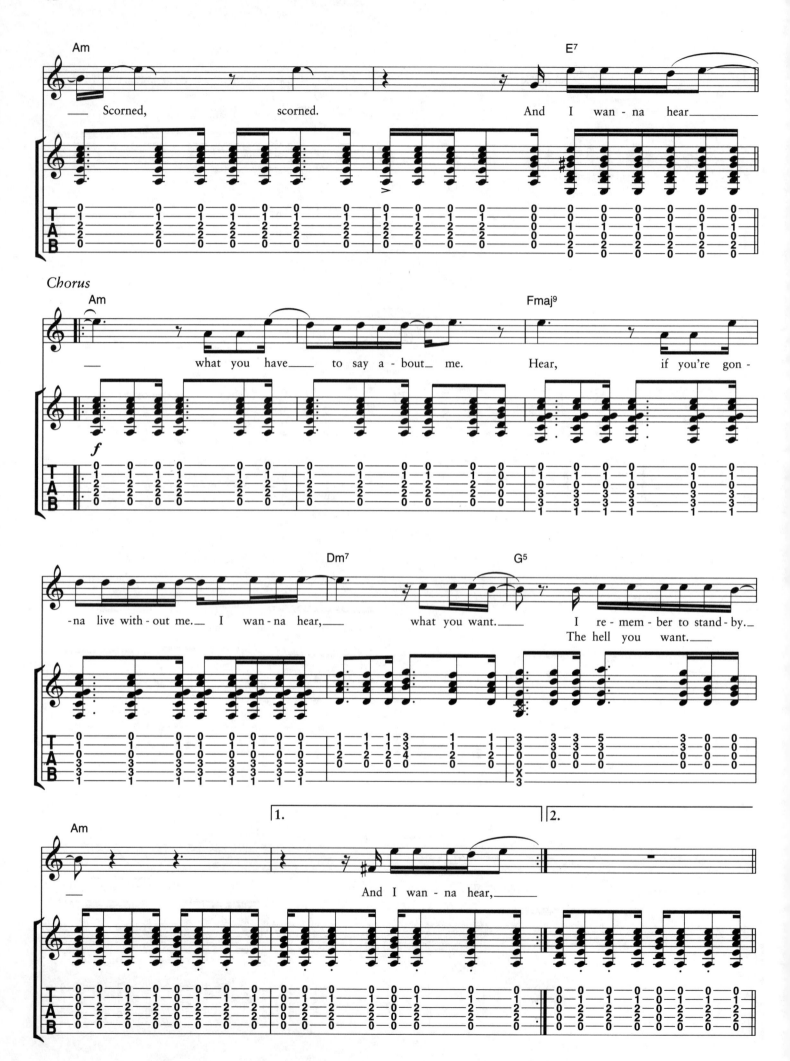

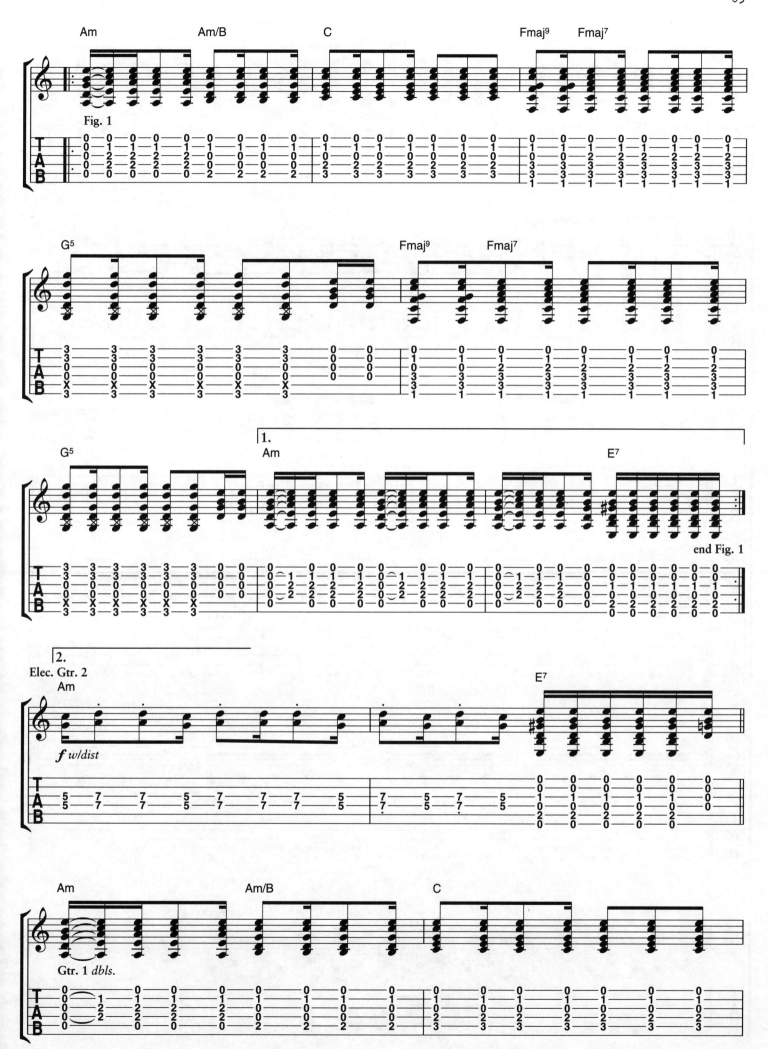

# eskimo

Words and Music by Damien Rice

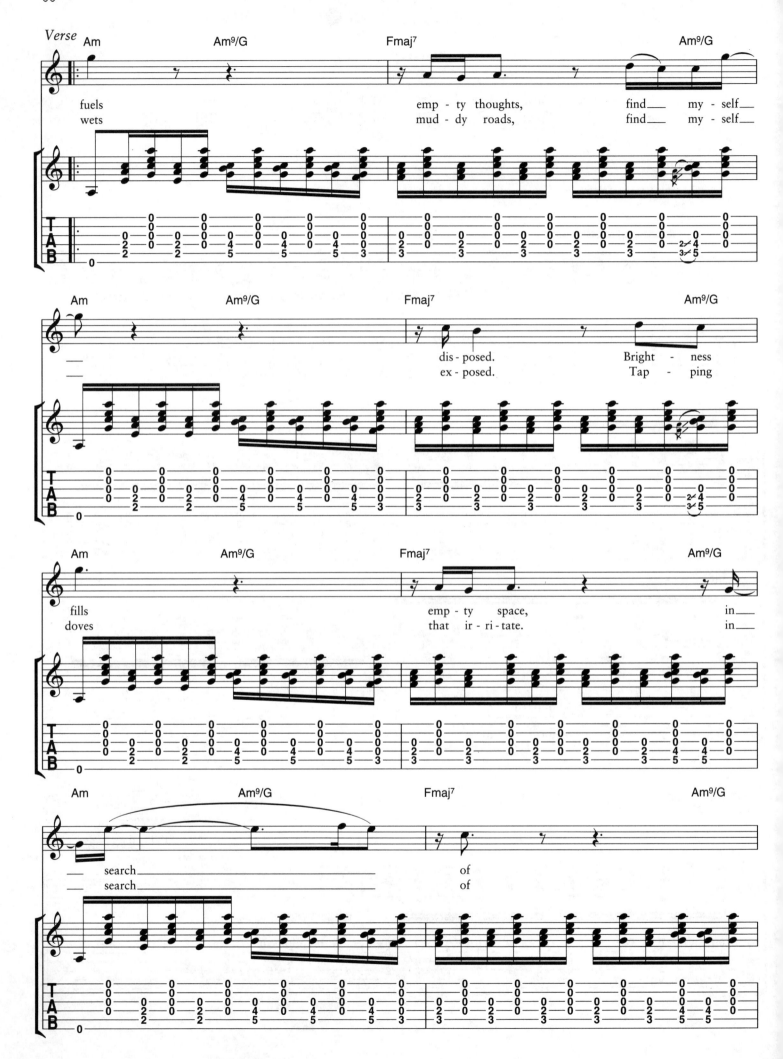

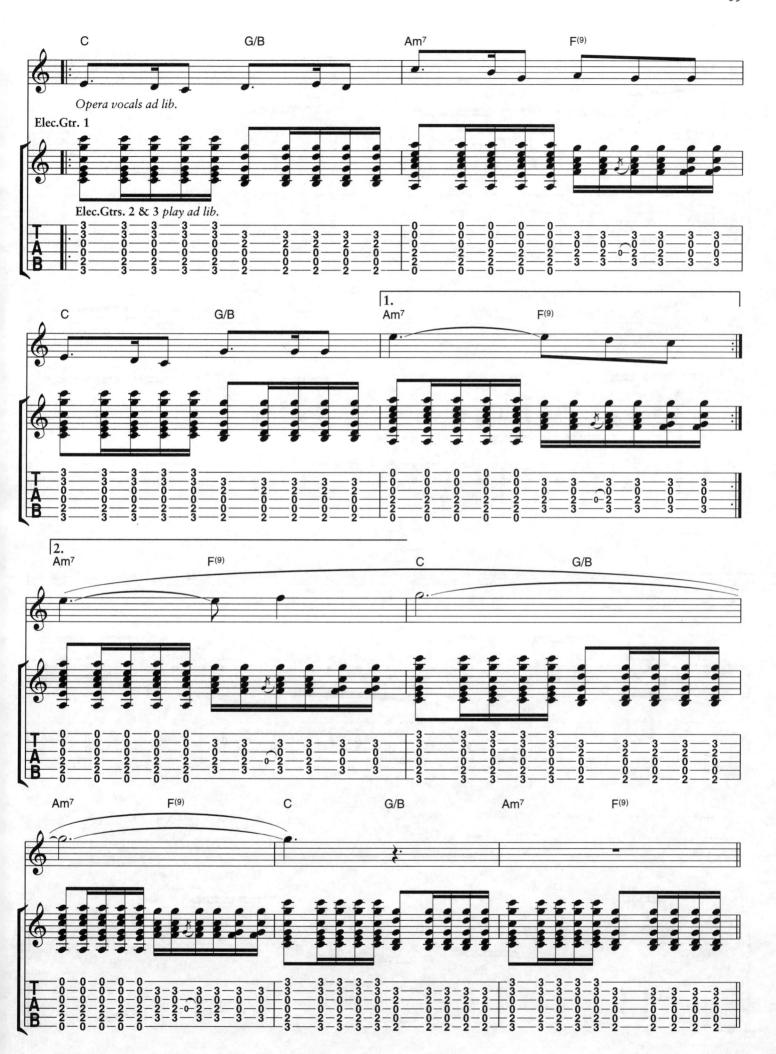

# prague

Words and Music by Damien Rice

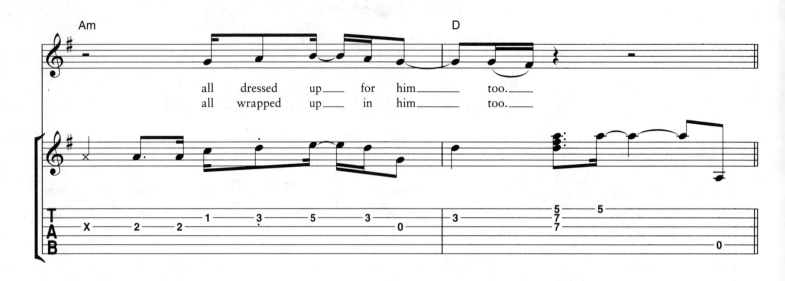

all   dressed   up___   for   him_____   too._____
all   wrapped   up___   in   him_____   too._____

*2nd time Gtrs 2,3+4 play ad lib.*

*Verse:*

Pre - pare my - self__ for a_____ war,
Pre - pare my - self__ for a_____ war,

Elec. Gtr. 1

Elec. Gtr. 4

*mp w/clean tone*

Fig. 1

end Fig. 1

Elec. Gtr. 2

*mf w/clean tone*
*Gtr. 3 dbls. ad lib.*

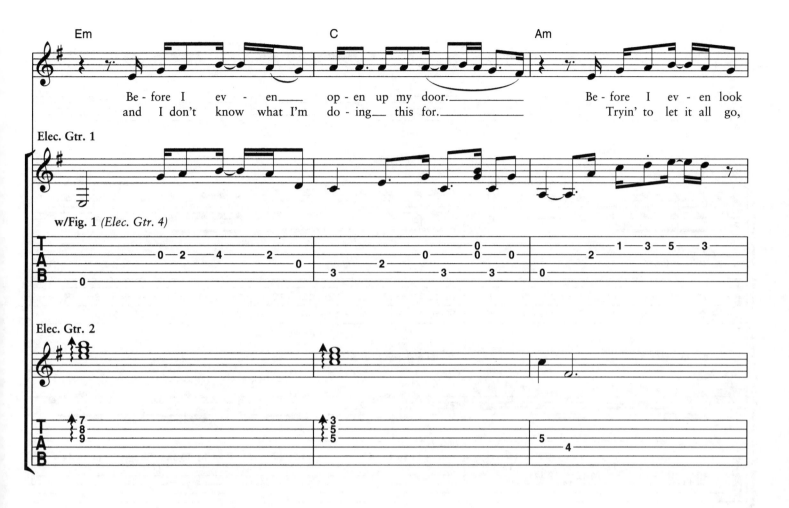

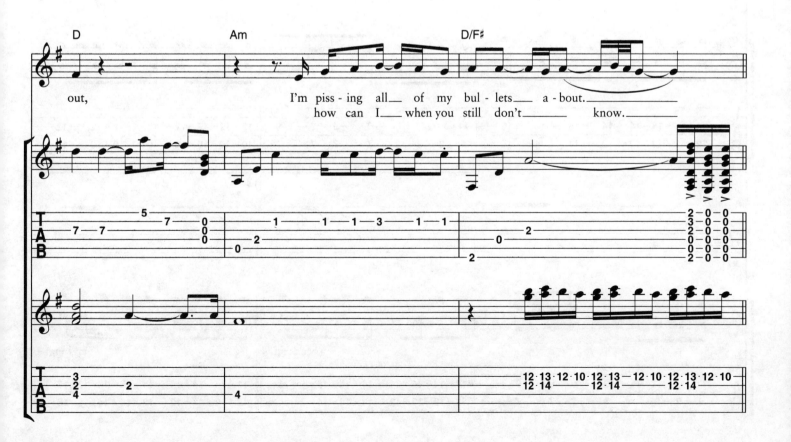

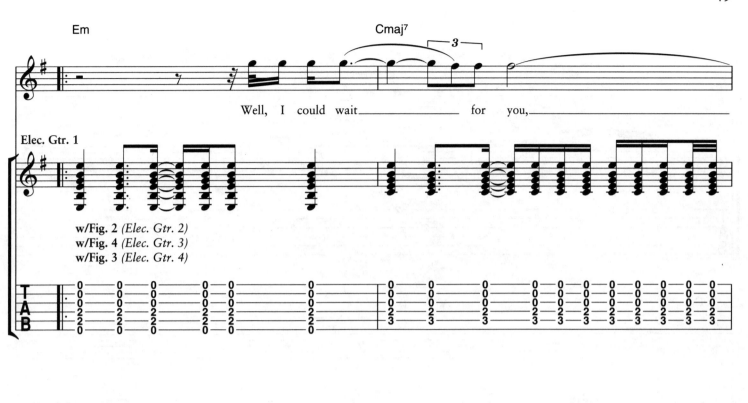

Well, I could wait_____ for you,_____

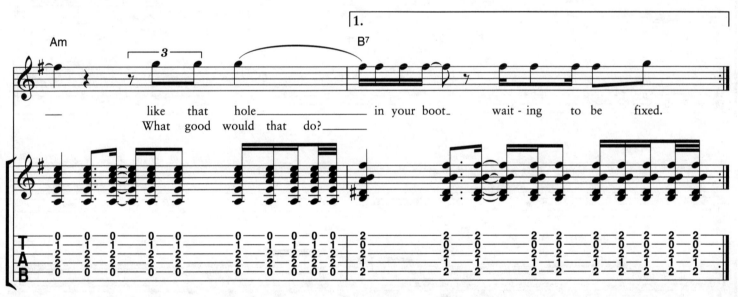

like that hole_____ in your boot_ wait-ing to be fixed.
What good would that do?_____

but to leave me pricked. Dar - lin',

# silent night

Traditional
Arranged by Lisa Hannigan

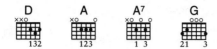

**Freely**

*Chorus* D *(chords implied)*

Si - lent night, bro - ken night.
Si - lent night, moon - lit night.

A    A7    D

All is fall - en when you take your flight.
No - thing's changed, no - thing is right.

*Verse:* G    231    D

I found some hate for you just_____ for show,
I should be strong - er, then weep - ing a - lone,

G    D

you found some love for me, think - ing I'd go. Don't
you should be weak - er than send - ing me home. I

A    A7    D

keep me from try - ing to sleep,_____
can't stop you fight - ing to sleep,_____

A7    1. D    2. D

sleep___ in___ hea - ven - ly peace.    peace.

# GUITAR TAB GLOSSARY**

## TABLATURE EXPLANATION

**READING TABLATURE:** Tablature illustrates the six strings of the guitar. Notes and chords are indicated by the placement of fret numbers on a given string(s).

*String* ⑥ 3rd *Fret*    *String* ① 12th *Fret*    A "C" Chord    "C" Chord Arpeggiated
*String* ③ 13th *Fret*

## BENDING NOTES

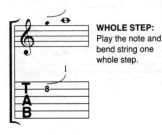

**HALF STEP:** Play the note and bend string one half step.*

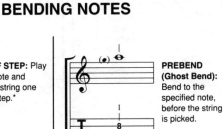

**WHOLE STEP:** Play the note and bend string one whole step.

**WHOLE STEP AND A HALF:** Play the note and bend string a whole step and a half.

**QUARTER-TONE BEND:** Play the note and bend string slightly to the equivalent of half a fret.

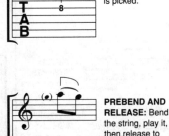

**PREBEND (Ghost Bend):** Bend to the specified note, before the string is picked.

**PREBEND AND RELEASE:** Bend the string, play it, then release to the original note.

**REVERSE BEND:** Play the already-bent string, then immediately drop it down to the fretted note.

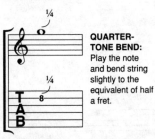

**BEND AND RELEASE:** Play the note and gradually bend to the next pitch, then release to the original note. Only the first note is attacked.

*A half step is the smallest interval in Western music; it is equal to one fret. A whole step equals two frets.

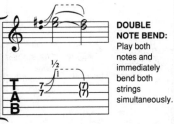

**UNISON BEND:** Play both notes and immediately bend the lower note to the same pitch as the higher note.

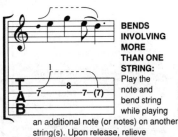

**DOUBLE NOTE BEND:** Play both notes and immediately bend both strings simultaneously.

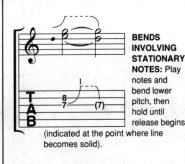

**BENDS INVOLVING MORE THAN ONE STRING:** Play the note and bend string while playing an additional note (or notes) on another string(s). Upon release, relieve pressure from additional note(s), causing original note to sound alone.

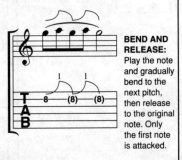

**BENDS INVOLVING STATIONARY NOTES:** Play notes and bend lower pitch, then hold until release begins (indicated at the point where line becomes solid).

## TREMOLO BAR

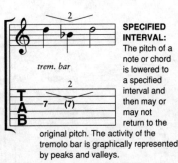

*trem. bar*

**SPECIFIED INTERVAL:** The pitch of a note or chord is lowered to a specified interval and then may or may not return to the original pitch. The activity of the tremolo bar is graphically represented by peaks and valleys.

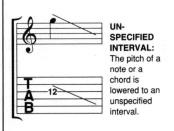

**UN-SPECIFIED INTERVAL:** The pitch of a note or a chord is lowered to an unspecified interval.

## HARMONICS

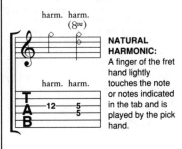

**NATURAL HARMONIC:** A finger of the fret hand lightly touches the note or notes indicated in the tab and is played by the pick hand.

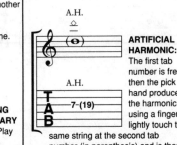

**ARTIFICIAL HARMONIC:** The first tab number is fretted, then the pick hand produces the harmonic by using a finger to lightly touch the same string at the second tab number (in parenthesis) and is then picked by another finger.

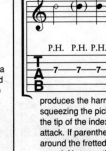

**ARTIFICIAL "PINCH" HARMONIC:** A note is fretted as indicated by the tab, then the pick hand produces the harmonic by squeezing the pick firmly while using the tip of the index finger in the pick attack. If parenthesis are found around the fretted note, it does not sound. No parenthesis means both the fretted note and A.H. are heard simultaneously.

**By Kenn Chipkin and Aaron Stang

80

## RHYTHM SLASHES

**STRUM INDICATIONS:** Strum with indicated rhythm. The chord voicings are found on the first page of the transcription underneath the song title.

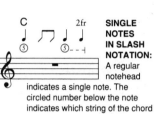

**SINGLE NOTES IN SLASH NOTATION:** A regular notehead indicates a single note. The circled number below the note indicates which string of the chord to strike. If the note is not in the chord, the fret number will be indicated above the note(s).

**FRETBOARD TAPPING:** "Tap" onto the note indicated by + with a finger of the pick hand, then pull off to the following note held by the fret hand.

**TAP SLIDE:** Same as fretboard tapping, but the tapped note is slid randomly up the fretboard, then pulled off to the following note.

**SHORT GLISSANDO:** Play note for its full value and slide in specified direction at the last possible moment.

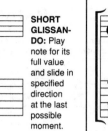

**PICK SLIDE:** Slide the edge of the pick in specified direction across the length of the string(s).

*pick sl.*

**TRILL:** Hammer on and pull off consecutively and as fast as possible between the original note and the grace note.

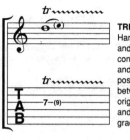

**ACCENT:** Notes or chords are to be played with added emphasis.

## ARTICULATIONS

**HAMMER ON:** Play lower note, then "hammer on" to higher note with another finger. Only the first note is attacked.

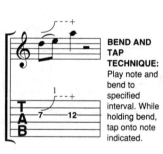

**BEND AND TAP TECHNIQUE:** Play note and bend to specified interval. While holding bend, tap onto note indicated.

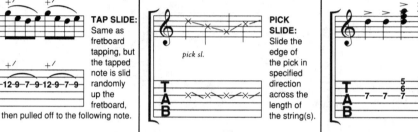

**MUTED STRINGS:** A percussive sound is made by laying the fret hand across all six strings while pick hand strikes specified area (low, mid, high strings).

low  mid.  high
stgs.  stgs.  stgs.

**STACCATO (Detached Notes):** Notes or chords are to be played roughly half their actual value and with separation.

**LEFT HAND HAMMER:** Hammer on the first note played on each string with the left hand.

**LEGATO SLIDE:** Play note and slide to the following note. (Only first note is attacked).

**PALM MUTE:** The note or notes are muted by the palm of the pick hand by lightly touching the string(s) near the bridge.

P.M.

**DOWN STROKES AND UPSTROKES:** Notes or chords are to be played with either a downstroke (⊓) or upstroke (ᴠ) of the pick.

**PULL OFF:** Play higher note, then "pull off" to lower note with another finger. Only the first note is attacked.

**LONG GLISSANDO:** Play note and slide in specified direction for the full value of the note.

**TREMOLO PICKING:** The note or notes are picked as fast as possible.

*trem. pick*

**VIBRATO:** The pitch of a note is varied by a rapid shaking of the fret hand finger, wrist, and forearm.